PARTY PEOPLE

Party People

MEG SEATON

HARRY CHAMBERS/PETERLOO POETS

First published in 1984
by Harry Chambers/Peterloo Poets
Treovis Farm Cottage, Upton Cross, Liskeard, Cornwall PL14 5BQ

ISBN 0 905291 64 6

Printed in Great Britain by
Latimer Trend & Company Ltd, Plymouth

ACKNOWLEDGEMENTS are due to the editors of *Candelabrum, City Limits, Envoi, Flying Crooked* (Stafford Poetry Society Anthology), *Imago* (Stafford Poetry Society Anthology), *New Poetry* (ed. Norman Hidden), *New Poetry 8* (Arts Council/PEN/Hutchinson, 1982), *New Poetry 9* (Arts Council/PEN/Hutchinson, 1983), *Other Poetry, Outposts, Poetry Matters, Tribune, Vision On* (Vers Poets), in whose pages some of these poems first appeared.

'Circus Christening' won 1st prize in the Scottish Open Poetry Competition, 1977.

'At Mozart's Funeral' won 2nd prize in the Scottish Open Poetry Competition, 1976.

'Landscape With Figure' won 1st prize in the Long Eaton Arts Festival Open Poetry Competition, 1983.

'When Peace Came' won 1st prize in Hornsey CND Peace Poem Competition, 1982.

'Henry' won 2nd prize in the Crabbe Memorial Competititon, 1982.

Cover photograph: Charles Dickens and his daughters, courtesy of National Portrait Gallery.

SUBSIDISED BY THE
Arts Council
OF GREAT BRITAIN

For Nina, my best person.

Contents

Party People

After the war he lingered on
dashing and sallying through the air
on various employment.

She in her flinty cottage
dabbling and daubing welcomed
his ton-up forays from the flying field.

Then, he demobbed, she pregnant,
hugely amused they married,
called their friends and neighbours.
Artists and airmen, fishermen,
babies and wives spilled joy
in rowdy sound from disapproving walls
far over the inimical North Sea.

Their legend went before them into Hampstead.
They were the party people.

Through thirty years it grew.
Birth, marriage, death, any excuse or none.
No need for baby-sitters, bring the kids,
we'll all mix in and carry memories
beyond the hangovers of splendid warmth
laced with improbable good fellowship.

It fell apart.
Their children grew and scattered.
Restless he flew to Rio,
died in the bed of some too lithe senora.

She stayed in her own corner, let out rooms,
her pictures smudgy now, unsaleable,
ghost laughter on the stairs.
Her unspayed cat teeming with kittens
gives raucous parties in the tangled garden.

Landscape With Figure

My aunt was a lover of landscape.
A hill and a puddle of water
reflecting the sun gave her pleasure.
Look, look, she would say, *at the pattern*
of clouds drifting over the mountains—
look, look at the lake surface rippling—
rejoice in the prospect before us.

Though bored by her artless reaction
I should have responded more warmly.
I left her, perhaps, chilled in spirit,
less satisfied with the excursion.

The day that I left her forever
the train rattled into a valley
soaked through with the waters of autumn,
the sky, grey as grief, hanging heavy,
leaves flaring like funeral torches,
turned earth black but promising harvest,
grass holy as jade, ever-living,
though she would make no more excursions.

At Swan Lake

Great Aunt Eliza swam out of the past,
light as a leaf, with a questing nose,
bilberry eyes and wire-wool wig.
tripping upon the neatest of feet,
dipping among the cygnets.

Never in life had she entered the door
of theatre or concert hall, that would be sin
though, avid for ha'pence, she'd sit up till two
in the morning at cards.

Great Aunt Eliza was born quite devoid
of fancy or fantasy. She simply *knew.*
God was a person who, out of a cloud
tethered just over the chapel, advised
on such problems as choosing a dress.

Why does Eliza, compact of plain sense,
trainer of maid-servants, coddler of hens,
partaker of gossip, wave plump, pretty feet
over the dancers in tutus and tights?

Why does she haunt me, disturb my appraisal of
fouettés and entrechat, jetés and jumps?
She would dispel the frail world of the swan-girls,
call it *a silly tale*. She would be right.

Sailor

How long ago?

More than a hundred years.
He was your grandad's grandfather, you know.
His mother died when he was six years old.

And did he cry?

There would be tears.
So much remains untold.
Well-spoken, willing, trim,
at twelve he ran away,
shipped as a cabin boy, his letters say.

But why?

Oh, who can tell?
The sea encompassed him,
the brutish sea, its snarl his lullaby.
Sharp-slapping sail,
water and wind and sky
seasoned him well.
Teak hard and timber dry
he found odd harbourage between each gale,
for three decades scorched, froze
and then came home.

What did he bring?
A mermaid's comb?

Who knows?
A sea-salt thirst, tanned skin,
a knife scar down his side,
a coral spray, a ring—
but still within
his heart, so said his bride,
a gentleness. His mother's gift.
Who died.

Conjuror

His is an ancient art.
Nodding across millennia to Moses,
winking at Belteshazzar and his rivals
stiff in Chaldean robes,
sideways he glances at Pythagoras.
Nearer, his smile proclaims complicity
with Dr. Dee, some sympathy
for Nostradamus.

He is benign.
No evil emanations
spark from his fingertips.
This skill is all his own,
no blood-signed bond was made
with Mephistopheles.

He wraps us in the warmth of his large presence
touches us with a nimble spirit,
holds us with lively eyes,
compelling acquiescence.
Conditioned, we rock with joy,
our senses caught in yards of coloured silks,
coins pouring from our ears,
bewildered by a spate of flying cards,
charmed by a dance of dishes,
happily deceived.

He breaks the spell and sends us shuffling out
into inimical night
but lighted by—until the oil gives out—
a magic lamp.

Bereft, he lingers in the empty hall
empty of virtue.

Circus Christening

The Bishop has arrived in his robes.
  Splendour was called for.
The swathes of violet,
  the thin coin of his face,
    give him a stained glass image.

His chaplain disapproves in dark grey.
    He carries the stoup.

The canvas of the big top flaps in the wind,
  a summoning sound.
    The ring is deep in sawdust, the air heavy
      with forgotten forests.

They, too, are in full costume.
  Bra and bikini sparkle
    above red boots.
      Lurex and diamanté
        glitter like tropical fish.
          The clown turns cartwheels,
            whorls of white and scarlet.

The lady of the birds brings her doves.
  The ripple of their wings recalls
    the Paraclete.
The liberty horses, held in decorous pairs,
  are lost in dreams of oats.
    Elephants watch with gravity
      and, from their cages,
        lions contribute organ music.

The spangled juggler and his high wire wife
   present their daughter.
Secure in her milieu
   she accepts the Bishop
      as just another clown
         and does not cry
            at touch of holy water
nor when the godmother
   completes the rite
      with a light dab of greasepaint
         and a sprinkle of sawdust
            dropped in the curled-shell palm.

She is equipped.

Ghost Train

It was an undertaking.
Corner seat, booked in advance,
back to the engine,
luncheon basket ordered
(chicken and ham,
lettuce like frosty mornings,
crusted rolls),
cologne at hand,
lace hanky for the smuts,
a snug, light rug
and sixpences for tips.

Much talk of connections,
fears that things might be
difficult at Crewe
(where a man hanged himself
and who can wonder?),
God-speeds and Give-my-loves—

Bustle—a slam of doors,
obsequious porters
pocketing their pelf,
the glimpse of a green flag.

No count-down but a
pterodactyl scream
slices the day.
Hissing, the jointed snake
jerks into life,
grumbles and thumps,
gains power,
achieves its rhythm,
moves irrevocably
forward into the past.

Wife To Albert

A little woman, bound about with flesh,
avid at table, eager in his arms
though much resenting the inevitable
result of the seclusion of the bed.
She shook with childlike laughter, wept with ease,
propounded sentiments of moral weight,
chilled many hearts with deep disapprobation
and, sharp with anger, quarrelled now and then
in private with the one she most adored.

She ruled her realm (with able ministers),
spoke sensibly, preserved the status quo
and kept, against all odds, a dignity
which vanquished enemies and left such friends
as protocol allowed on the far side
of ice-floes that hemmed in the ship of state.

She had been lucky in her chosen prince,
a man of elegance and rectitude,
excited by new wonders of the age,
an amateur of music, just a shade
too rigid in his views, too humourless
to win the larky English but *so true*.

He tired in twenty years. The typhoid germs
found easy prey. Shaking portentous beards
the ineffectual physicians watched
his fractious, fevered death.

For forty years
Regina et Imperatrix still trod
the deck and watched while the surrounding ice
encroached still further till it froze her heart.

Victoriana

Walls ascending into darkness,
curtains drawn against the prowling evening,
lamp and bedside candle-shaded,
seven children brought through pools of shadow
say goodbye to Mamma.

Fourteen eyes absorb images to be
crystalised in each memory.
Papa's watchchain, caught in candlelight,
entrances Paul, a future preacher
Who will one day see
the coveted bauble among earthly fetters.
Grave sailor-suited Arthur only watches
the unfamiliar landscape of the loved face
pale on the pillow. Agnes is scandalised
by small Jane's apple bottom, neat in cambric
frilled at the edges, as abandoned
she throws herself across the bed.
And is removed.
She sees the rosy thrust of the midwife's nose.
Emily tracks the pattern of the quilt,
takes in a wandering smell,
It is Dr. Simpson's blessed anodyne,
sanctified by the queen.
Emmy herself will come to know it well.
Harry, prone to night fears, calls up dragons,
shapes flung by fluttering fire.
Emmy's neat wheaten plait tempts Susan's fingers.

Papa is led away by Aunt Eliza.
Robust, he will survive.

Mamma is a long way off. She is not concerned
for the seven pillars of nature's wisdom
nor for the infant weeping by the fire.
She has climbed a tree and is hanging on for life,
stuck in a fork, a fresh wind in her hair.
Lor, what a tomboy, Miss.

Dickie will help her down, her favourite brother,
not that plump man who talked the other day
of bears and bulls and gilts—such farmyard stuff.
Oh lovely to be young, your body free, unclaimed,
Yours to enjoy alone.
She must let go. Dickie will catch her.
Now.

Diamond Jubilee Baby

Swaddled, impressive in a goffered bonnet,
warmly enshrouded in a wool pelisse,
bounded by the hood of a bassinet
eased through the park by Mother's guiding hand
(they did not all have nannies),
lying entranced in limbo till discomfort
seeping through dream recalled the living flesh
under the trappings, outraged he raised a cry.

Later, a flannel nightrobe hung to warm
on the high guard around the dancing fire.
Cot blankets well tucked in, the window closed,
(she would not let an air blow coldly on him)
Pussy, the daytime playmate, sent away,
Fido restrained, a lullaby sung softly
(just off the note) rounded a placid day.

So much of love, so much of cherishing
gave confidence when needed to withstand
six of the best, playground indignities,
a father's stern injunctions;
gave the inspired assurance for his spring
towards the spitting guns before he lay
tangled in wire, a rag, in No-Man's-Land.

She would die too you thought but with much pride
and quiet melancholy she enshrined
his medal from the king.

English Eccentric

(*Mary Kingsley, traveller and trader, 1861–1900*)

Miss Kingsley's spirit was abroad.

Now all the fighting cocks in England stirred.
They lifted beaks and spiked the sky
with crooked cries of homage.

Inimical rocks stood harsh and blind
as soldiers passed through Simonstown
convoying useless skin and bone
on a gun carriage down to the sea.

There warships waited.
A salute was fired.
A grim, grand exit.

Far northward an enquiring presence moved
about the huts where sleep made innocence
of savagery. Witch doctors sprang awake
calling for fire and ululation,
praise and pervading drums. Noise equals life.
The friendly ghost in old fur hat
and long dark cannibal-resistant skirt
was honoured but howled out to silent limbo.

Somewhere a leopard growled, hair stiffening,
for she had been a legend in their order.

The mangrove swamp was troubled.
Paddles plashed in the dark.
Here she had come to seek identity,
alone to find herself in greater loneliness,
to see her own face in the secret face
of Africa.

A solitary lady and endearing.
We do not want her back.

Forbearing missionaries, politicians,
the palm oil trading ruffians, her peers,
for once agreed.

Remembering A Garden In Johannesburg

A scatter of petals patterns a Joseph coat
in colours of blood and cream and afterglow.
Do not arraign the roses or, about their roots
in royal velvet, pansies, dark as Piet himself
who monitors their need of mulch and water.
They also work, to charm the necessary bee.
Mesembryanthemums, flung like a child's bright chain
across the low wall, flaunt their paintbox innocence.
Beyond my windowsill the poinsettia flares
proclaiming poison, subtle as a demon king.
The bougainvillea, trellised splashes magenta
against the morning, hiding among its leaves
a swivel-eyed chameleon, darting death to flies.
Here is no colour bar,
                                        Wash-day brings Susannah,
archetypal matriarch swaying along the drive
in splendour of warm brown flesh, bundle on head,
a trail of pregnant daughters in her wake,
equipped with antique patience for the ironing board,
their voices atavistically attuned
to bridging tracts of sky from hill to Zulu hill.

Susannah sees me at the rubbish bin. *Oh Ma'am,*
the earth-voice coaxes, *don't throw away the flowers.*
I take them to the cemetery—is all right—
the dead people won't know they are finished too.

I hope I gave her fresh ones. I have forgotten
but over the years, over six thousand miles,
Susannah I remember, the roses and Piet,
the plum-flesh of his arms absolving Tretchikoff.
All finished, maybe, like the dead people's flowers,
the roses sacrified to make a tennis court—
Susannah—Piet—in their Soweto homes—?

Bush Hospital

Here on the edge of the bush
night drops a blanket
dousing the flaring day,
killing our comfortable shadows.

Light in the white doctor's room
flickers, obscured
by a frisson of wings,
by smoke. The cistern drips.

He is alone with Africa.

In the large sky
each star is solitary.

Only the crickets
in scrub, in thorn,
scrape out a message of love.

Now from the witch doctor school
across the veldt
comes a shudder of drums
filling the dark
with ghostly impis,
with lemurian wailing.

Life was a grain in this soil
before time was born.

Here the first hominid
rose upright,
freeing his hands
for mischief.

Here the last man
may stumble
to bequeath his bones to dust.

There will be silence.

After millennia
first an uncertain cricket
then a drum.

Poor Man

He should never have left the cave;
packed earth against his bone
a hard assurance,
starfish profusion of limbs,
flung out, curled, mingled, furry,
the air a presence
thick with old food,
old faeces, friendly flesh,
fire at the entrance
living charm against
the flash of sabre tooth,
the blundering mammoth.

But he crept out,
observed the night,
stars tangled in his hair,
moon in his eyes,
stumbled,
found Eden,
lost it,
lost the cave
forever.

Poor man.
Poor man.

Tell It As It Was

His shadow came before him.

Children whipped into the cave,
rolled to the women's feet,
pointing with bloody fingers
(they were killing
some small creature
in the dust).

Hunting in dream
men leapt awake,
turned, gripped their spears,
faced into day.

He came, his hands extended
holding nothing but his life.

His stink was different,
the skins he wore were strange.
They gave him meat.
They gathered.

There was a man
who rode a tree trunk
on the waters. . . .

Peering with fire-bright eyes
through mats of hair,
the children.

Tell it as it was.

Bouncing and bounding
down the centuries
the words re-echo.

When Peace Came

Now it was over.
Heads of state emerged
into the tested air.
(They had sent out doves.)

There were not many.
Six or eight perhaps
from each once-warring country,
improbably bronzed—
the sun-lamps had worked well.

The treasured cars,
deep buried under lead
with brimming tanks,
were brought to light,
the journeys made
through plains of ash
and dust and a few black bones
like twigs; but there were no trees.

The sky was grey as though
the cloud still lingered.
There was no sound
except a sobbing wind.

They met and fell
upon each other's necks
feeling an unexpected surge
of love for things that lived.

It would be peace
forever now.
Staggering on uncertain feet
they knew that they had made
their final territorial demands.

Dialogue

Grandma
how long will you live?

Look through the window.
While the sight of the sun
staining and changing
patterns of autumn leaves
moves me to ponder
light and its nature
life will be strong.

You might go blind.

Memory paints old masters.
While I recall
the contour of your cheek,
the gravity of your gaze
I shall live.

But you might—

So I might.
Over the years
I shall enter you
now and then
in the tone of a voice,
a movement, a touch.
I shall live richly in you.

Will you live till the bomb?

A Tabulated Numerical Fact

Madam,
your child is a statistic,
a tabulated numerical fact.

I should be proud.

One of two out of five thousand,
Four thousand nine hundred and ninety eight
will benefit from the inoculation.

I know only one child,
whose eyes showed trust and curiosity,
whose fingers were explorers, testing the world,
whose mind was unfolding like a leaf bud.

A compensatory payment may be made.

What compensation for a crystal bowl,
unique and precious,
rayed with spreading flaws,
doomed to disintegrate?

Henry

Quick fish, too curious,
he leapt too soon
from amniotic waters.
He should have dreamed
another hundred days
in the alchemic dark
where seed, transmuting,
learns its code.

A flutter of flying gowns
obscures his altar.
Enclosed, controlled,
no bigger than a hand,
his thread of fire
endlessly tended
by masked acolytes,
science in his strict service
is benign.

The flame grows stronger.
He acquires personage,
black-pansy eyes observe,
the walnut skin is sleek.
Thin as the paws
of harvest mice
his fingers
retain their hold on being.

(* *Henry weighed twenty-three ounces at birth but survived*)

Nina In Dudgeon

(*aged two years, one month and nine days*)

Small Queen Victoria
trundled in chair,
upright,
tragically unamused,
puffed cheeks pale,
washed eyes red-rimmed,
one gripped daisy
held erect, a sceptre.

I would charge
the clouds
on a lightning horse
to bring you down
the sun,

I would give you
my last joy.

Nina's Story

ANNUNCIATION

Candles on the table
and a trail of berries,
October dusk shrinking the shadowed room,
masking the angel.
Her hands in the splash of light
dispensing bread and wine,
grace that she shared with legendary queens
deepened by chthonic wisdom,
by the leap at the heart of the earth
at the promise of the winter solstice.
Amazed, we bent our heads
before the smile that silenced Joseph.

BIRTH

When, most improbably,
those microscopic travellers
touched, locked, absorbed each other
you were at once an entity, quick fish
flicking your tail in amniotic waters,
achieving personage, impelled
to tunnel forward to the astounding light.

DIVORCE

They held you in a citadel of love
until with time the outworks fell,
the garrison defected,
a fresh command moved in.

Remember, always, mutability,
a shifting pattern of parents,
a complication of siblings,
cannot diminish you who were Revelation,
their first, most treasured, hoard
of Inca gold.

The Ophelia Syndrome

Mask reality with grace.
Wash the witness from its face.
Turn a grin of mortal stress
to favour and to prettiness.
Charm to quell a silent scream,
take a savaged rib as theme
for grave and lovely lullabies
to close death-darkened eyes.

Seared by everlasting frost,
scattered skulls, their masters lost,
are indifferent to the plough,
flesh that housed them nothing now.

Tell of *warriors who sleep*.
In poppied symbolism keep
their festival. Let legends flow
around them like transforming snow.

The grieving dog that howls alone
knows that bone is only bone.

Music For A Boy King

He is buried in gold
to hold him forever,
his essence unspilled
into time, the fell river,
his majesty held
by the skillful engraver,
his spirit revealed
as a feathered sky rover.

Among the farrago
surrounding the Pharaoh,
the lapidary's yield,
the goldsmith's endeavour,
a small image tooled
by a cunning wood carver,
the work of a lover,
the gift of a griever,
recalls the lost child.

His nurse, old deceiver,
has smoothed down the cover,
has soothed him and lulled
the terrors that hover
in shadow, and stilled
the dimmed mind of its fever.

And now it is over.

A Pharaoh Dies

In this high room gaudy with painted pillars,
lit by squared inlets under the flowered roof,
exuberance of day droops into shadow.

Heat is a giant presence, dominant,
hymned by a choir of flies
rampant as slaves drowse standing.

Nothing of royalty here:
fever-dried flesh, a wandering pain, a whimper.
He is young,
the old nurse vigilant,
the girl wife crumpled near him.

Beyond the walls the whips of the sun
lash the unflinching back of a fisherboy,
lazy beside the Nile.
Sores on his skin, sharp-boned,
his belly full of worms,
he sucks a honey sweet, grins, is content.

A wail seeps from the palace,
thin as a sickle, keen as a hunting knife,
forlorn defiance of the ice-footed newcomer,
cold-shouldering thief of light.
Edges of silence, ripped, waver together,
fuse then are torn again by lamentation.

Time, the still sea, lies all around.
He has floundered into aeons.

He will be lapped in gold,
the cobra writhing, watchful, at his head
for three millennia
before unloving hands
uncover his last mysteries.

The fisherboy, one with the river mud,
will suffer less indignity.

Not About A Cat

The small cold lakes
reflecting yellow moon
absorb them. Pulling out
half hypnotised
they ask if the breed is rare.

The M above his eyes
proclaims true tabby,
also implies much mingling.
Some British Longhair,
touch of Siamese,
a rout of alley toms
went to his making.
With long front legs
that hint at Pharaoh's
jewelled hunting cats
he treads his mongrel footprints
back through millennia
but knows himself a god.

The use of the dismissive tailflick
humbles them
for they are citizens
of the second class.

Had they been taken up,
raised from their bulrushes
to dwell in purple,
nourished on fatlings,
every wish fulfilled
by watchful slaves,
they too would walk like gods.

Double Helix

(*After Miroslav Holub's 'A Boy's Head'*)

Inside a cat's head
is
an undiminishable fish,
a patch of portable sunlight,
warm not hot,
a titillating flutter of feathers,
a provocative, dangling string.

Nightmare, there is a fog
of flying flea powder.

There is a hand touching,
sometimes in the right place,
sometimes in the wrong.

Left over from the Wild
is a coiling thread of suspicion.
Justified.
There is, alas, no sex.

* * *

Inside a cat's head
is
the image of a she-cat
just below the tail,
dustbins with juicy content,
an unguarded chop,
feet to be avoided,
weather, which is important.

There are teeth, claws,
a spitting tangle of fur.
There is a rolling array of roof tops,
All his.

Double Life

I am the one who waits by the telephone,
who watches the postman pass,
who spends the day devising
the perfect meal
for guests who forget to come,
who treads the nettlepatch
of small annoyances,
about whose ears
a buzz of worry is perpetual,
who lives, lined, dried and bent,
with little griefs.

I, too, am she
who drifts among cool shoals
of sempiternal peace,
who pulses with the music of the planets,
who reads the book of the sea.

I am the oyster,
secret as the womb,
who cherishes a pearl.

Brother Eadric In The Orchard

Brother Eadric walked in the orchard,
drank the blossom, drank the grass,
took great draughts of the washed sky,
sucked the sun dry,
pierced by singing voices.

Cold as water, kiss of stone
chilled his body as he lay
worn by fasting, seared by scourging,
many nights by the cross to pray.

Only the Abbot knew him pagan.
Not for him the sacred acre.
Weaker brethren, wondering, whispered,
digging deep in unhallowed earth.

Passing through the shadowed cloisters
novices hymned the holy birth
while the long bones of Brother Eadric
buried under an apple tree
wore a weight of snow, a shrouding
splendour of austerity.

High rise flats where trampling northmen
burned the abbeys, felled the orchard,
hold no echo of the music
Eadric heard with ravished soul
but some neighbour child may be
speared by his ghostly ecstacy.

At Mozart's Funeral

That day in Vienna
the cloak of dignity
fell finally to pieces.
It had been frayed before,
snagged by a hundred
barbed humiliations.

Like cavalry the wind
scattered the gathered friends.
They gave before
the sabres of the sleet.
They needed wine and fire.
The man was dead.
They could not help him now.

All right for him—he's snug.
Shovel it in—
who would dig graves in winter,
earth like rock—and for a pauper?
Shovel it in
before my nose drops off
from cold.

And they too left.

Dark came.
The intricacies of snow,
each flake a symphony
of ordered particles,
clustered above him.

Silence. The beat,
the all pervading rhythm
checked at last.
The man was dead.

Ours is the music.

After Mozart

(*A few days later when Constanza came*
they could not find the grave.)

A fitted sky like a pale china lid
enclosed the wind,
churned mud and dabbled snow.
The desolation of the pauper patch
where through misunderstanding and the storm
they'd buried him dismayed
the friends, too nearly touched
by bony fingers of mortality,
feet chilled in slush.
She wept and left.
There were the warm, live children.
There would be another marriage.

It could not matter that the foolish flesh
anonymously rotted into earth.
The peacock child,
the pet of queens,
had perished long ago. The insolent youth had merged
into the married man
who found relief in much frivolity
from more humiliation.

So the effacing mud.
The debts were paid.

Reflecting light
the music leaps and bubbles,
scattering suns and moons,
proclaiming everlasting congruence.

A Beethoven Lodging

The walls have drawn in emanations
from former tenants, shadows,
echoes of voices, laughter.
They came and went.
The room is neutral,
it was never home.

He brought his luggage,
lightning in a cage,
rug-muffled thunder,
a hatbox full of gales,
his pockets stuffed with meteors.

Soon the room raged.
He loosed the tempest,
battered the keyboard of the abused piano,
shouted aloud in fury, hearing nothing.
Crochets and quavers crawled
the undulating walls.
The floor heaved,
stars beat against the ceiling
like trapped birds.

The landlord shuddered.

He did not stay.
Encompassed by the snows of silence
he stormed the warm and coloured world of sound
by moving three doors higher up the street.

The room resumed its shabby dignity,
stoically awaited further onslaughts.
Tourists arrived in droves and simple pilgrims
who hoped perhaps that genius left contagion.

A Picture by Jack Yeats

Under the landscape of a patchwork quilt
with fields of colour, contours of his bones,
he was surprised in sleep, his eyes still sealed,
his head hard back against the pillow,
chin and nose outlined with greater clarity
than in life, cheeks shadowed valleys.

The room is bare.
A plant in a pot on the sill
is occupied in nourishing new leaves.
A heavy matter.

Outside the window day has come and spring
shows in a washed blue sky, some greening branches.
Imagination brings into the frame
sounds of abounding life, the lark's bright chain
swung high above his nest, an ugly chatter
of fighting sparrow, half a feathered ounce
of animosity,
the bray of an ass, a cart grumbling over stones,
the impertinent whine of flies.

No noise can enter
this abandoned dwelling
so lately tenanted by one
as disputatious as the sparrows.
Here knowledge stops.
Only the atoms dance
through an inanity of peace.

Carpenter

He knows the truth of wood,
the arabesques of the grain,
the sensuous surfaces
revealed by the plane,
love-wounds forgiven now.

He is surrounded by lost forests
where in aromatic sleep the air
hangs among boughs,
where drinking mosses cling
wet-mouthed to earth,
where miracles of curling fern occur
and ivy inches out tenacious life
harbouring armies of hair-footed things.
Thicket and branch are set with eyes
aware as sentinels.
Trees, sucking at the soil,
vibrate like wires.

The forests fallen
honest wood is all their immortality.
The wood proclaims responsibility,
the carpenter accepts his guilt, his glory.

The anonymity of plastic
did not achieve the cross.
It was his own inevitable work.

Censure For Romantics

A rose never knows and a doe cannot know,
no more can long dead Romeo,
that a flower cupping dew or a deer's dark eye
or a tale of lovers dead in the long gone by
may run you through
        like a sword,
            like a shivering sword
                that cuts your rose-red heart in two.

A rose never knows that a rose is red,
a doe cannot see her gentle head
and dust cannot weep for bright blood shed
        in the glare,
            in the glare,
                in the glittering glare
                    of strident sun and thin bright air.

Why should you care for a careless thing?
a petal lip, a leaf in spring,
a trembling lake where moonshafts drown
may start a river rolling down
from your eyes
        from your eyes
            from your washed red eyes
                where salt in sad abundance lies.

O save your salt to savour your wit.
One day you may have need of it.

Down From The Moon

If the old friar had sent a quicker messenger
would Juliet have ridden from Verona,
memory shadowed, daunted by a glimpse
of something less than pleasant
that lately was her glittering cousin Tybalt,
the fruit of that one night,
sharp with spiked stars,
already setting in her petalled centre
and then, no doubt, a dirty inn,
leers from the landlord, sniggers from his wife,
no brash, familiar nurse to comfort her?
All of her fourteen years would hang on her
like iron rings.

They would at first find lodging with some aunt,
some widowed, mad contessa—
no hint of kitchen sink but she would cry,
mourning her home as he would mourn
his golden sheaf of friends.
Her face would sharpen and her tongue,
her figure thicken.
With beauty's ensign drooping at half mast
he would remember Rosalyne.
It could not last unless—
a miracle—
cooling hot blood with patience, they might win
in wisdom what they lost in rapture
and through eroding but rewarding years
cobble a rough, tough marriage.

The Moonies Told Her

The Moonies told her
   that the world
      will come to an end
         soon, soon.

She said
   that's all I'm short of.
      little Alfie whooping his heart out,
         the telly on the blink
            a summons for the rates
AND NOW THE END OF THE WORLD.

They did not tell her
   that with every breath she draws
      the world ends
         for someone,
            sun turns to ash,
               silence devours all sound,
                  a black hole sucks
                     like a child at some breast.

It might be more cosy
   if we all went
      hand in hand.

The Flower Child's Daughter

Dad was a flower child, poor old sod.
Locked in the loo, he chats to God.
He hasn't had fun it seems to me
since he gave up on LSD.
Mum tried to fly and took a dive
from the top of St. Paul's. She is not alive
but in the instant of her flight
her senses, surely, blazed with light.

Sometimes I wish that I had been
Old enough to share their scene.
Gran brought me up with my feet on the ground
although she, too, has been around
and often expatiates on her past, on
the days when she marched to Aldermaston
and carried a banner for CND,
fed to the teeth with victory.

So here am I with a life to live
for just as long as the war lords give
or cars or cancer cells allow.
I'm not sure where I'm standing now.
I don't like Libbers, I don't want to be
the single parent of a family.
I've got my O's and I've got my A's
but I don't want nine to five all my days.
I don't want the dole or wheeling deals.
I weep for whales and I sue for seals.
I reach for something I cannot see
and hear my mother calling me
but I'm glad to have known the human race
before it vanishes without trace.

Prospect Of Resurrection

Ash from Helen's pyre may mix with
nacre in the oyster's matrix.
Pearl, resultant, may not be
all her immortality.

Carried on a robber's sandal
out of phosphorescent gravelight
atoms that were Nefertiti
sail millennia of moonlight.

All of her that was uncomely
lost in smoke in Golders Green
something of old Mrs Bagshott
wreathes and spirals by at cockshut.

Whorls of time uncoil, uncover
numinous radiance at the core.
Atoms swirling into timelight
take the shapes that once they wore.

Living holograms in spacetime,
Helens may proliferate,
Nefertitis plague the planets,
supermarkets swarm with Bagshotts.

Stuff of life will change about
until the heart of time burns out.

Corner Shop

I blow in on a gritty wind.
The Cypriot, heavy and old
in English light, sits by the till.
Behind him mounded globes—
oranges, apples, tomatoes
and shining gold onions—
pulsate with colour.

I gather soap powder, biscuits and tea,
everything filmed with dust and stocks run down—
how can he hope to compete?

Slowly he lowers the dingy paperback.
I'm reading about Constantios. The Great.

And then he tells me.
We reach the point where St. Helena
mislaid her cross and lo! it arose in Cyprus.
Miracle!
He starts back in his chair,
hands and eyes raised, lips parted.
He sees the cross rampant against a sky
of raging blue.
I see it too.

I don't know how this book came in my house.

He remembers.

Four years ago I took the family to Rhodos
to see the butterflies.
You drive to Lindos and the butterflies—

His fingers flicker and I also see them,
a springing cloud of flowers taking flight.
And I see too
the watered silk of the Aegean
under the sun.

Seventy eight pence, eighty,
ninety, three pounds—

Cheap at the price.

East Suffolk Memories

The air, honed like a scythe,
sent us as high
as the frost-hardened blue.

But in the village
clustered cottages
were mean of window
and those small windows
always tightly shut.

Eyes peered out
under light lashes
and reddish hair,
the Danish legacy.
Along the street
abounded coughing cousins,
the foreigner unwelcome.

I went back.
The street was there,
the windows.
From one of them
eyes dark as mangrove swamps
stared out.
new blood had come
that long ago
in Africa was old.

Herrenvolk

Roman soldier
born in Nubia
dried in sunlight
died in marshlight
died of a fever
by London's river
buried deep in London clay.

Catuvellauni
girl, red-tawny,
caught in the reeds
on a ghost-grey day
found without roads
the Severn water
reared his elf-child
far away.

Saxon marauder
took the daughter
gave her another
with hair like hay
future breeder
of more bed-fodder,
fox-beard Dane and Norman prey.

Drinking deep
by London's river
pub-bound patriots
proudly pray
English keep us,
pure forever,
sink the rest in London clay.

Footnote People

Forgive us our trespasses
who briefly trod
on such clear shadows,
creeping along the edge
of a greater life.

We also lived
and moved in the bustle of day,
treasured our aspirations,
knew the thrust of death.

We scrabble, restless,
at the brink of memory.
To ourselves
we were not footnote people.
We usurped the page.

Perhaps you, too,
behind that mask
are marginal.

Assuage our ghosts
with sprigs of rosemary.

Meg Seaton is a freelance writer and script reader. She is a qualified drama teacher, but has had a variety of jobs and has wide interests. Born in London, with a mother connected with music and a father connected with magic. She has written short stories, children's stories and radio plays. Her verse output is minimal but has been persistent from the age of seven, sometimes with long gaps. *Party People* is her first full collection.